PATHS AND APPROACHES

Published in the United States by
Beckham Publications Group, Inc.
ISBN: 978-0-9833402-4-9

Library of Congress Control Number: 2011926719

PATHS AND APPROACHES

Michael Maiello

THE **Beckham**
PUBLICATIONS GROUP, INC.
Silver Spring

ACKNOWLEDGMENTS

I am grateful to the editors of the following periodicals for first publishing the poems listed:

Amulet: "Once Wise"

Conceit Magazine: "Birth Daze," "Graced," "This Morning"

Common Ground Review: "Berg"

The Freefall Review: "Hidden (Obviously)"

Lone Stars: "Anti-Matters," "Holocaust," "Stormed"

Northern Stars: "Gamboling"

The Pen: "Amen Again"

Poetry Protocol: "Air Born," "Solos," "Visual Realities," "Weathered," "Woodstock Revisited"

The Storyteller: "Unstrung"

Write On: "Beached," "Cold Wars," "Zen Flyby"

CONTENTS

PART ONE: QUESTS AND REQUESTS

PART TWO: AIRSCAPES

PART THREE: GOOD DAZE, BAD DAYS

PART ONE

QUESTS AND REQUESTS

AIR BORN

We may well be residual chaos
from the big bang of creation.
We may well be primal roadlessness,
going nowhere, nowhere gone.
Serial starsets shatter us
in bed.
Love: an interdependent co-arising
moment of extinction.
Your hands sign gently:
any beginning at all
will do.

VIRTUAL REALITIES

The reign of God is now but not yet.
His kingdom here but still coming.
Peace is being at peace with this.
My father, who never studied Zen,
knew instinctively, "the gardener
is the flower, sometimes."
Sensing the folly of explanations,
he watched me grow, waiting for us
both to bloom.

DISCONNECTED

Paratroops and paramours,
dismissed and disregarded,
wait for their telephones
to ring.
Surely, they must be needed
somewhere.
This July, fireworks
and land mines sound
the same.
Circling the sun, I question
independence, humming
dial tone songs
about interest rates
and freedom.
A time will come
when service is restored.

AMEN AGAIN

We have Navajo death (beer)
and Apache death (scotch and beer).
We have dead seas, rights and reckonings.
We have the smell of leaf bonfires
and the bourbon smell of men
(and all the ice we need).
We have the inheritance to which
we'll all return.
There are birds that circle overhead
from beyond when we remember.
And still it seems the saddest thing
is lacking.

WEATHERED

The prayer of the wind,
the heaven of the wind,
a place where all things
are removed.

BERGS

In Greenland, I witnessed the indifference
of glaciers and the uselessness of ice
without whiskey.
I'm over fifty now and don't dream very much
about women or war anymore.
I find I have developed an abiding love
of evening.
Evening is the consequence of mercy.
I take the finality of each one to heart
as we both work on melting away.

GRAVE CONCERNS

All the angels have evaporated, more fallout
from global warming.
I'm looking at an icon of St. Michael, hoping
it didn't hurt him to disappear.
From a cabin in the Catskills, I can see
the Milky Way.
Am I really part of it and also in New York?
The late news reports anger in town
because fun is not the answer
to life's questions.
Before retiring, I'll search the area
for weapons of mass destruction.

SOLOS

The wind speaks
to itself, exulting
in the company
it keeps.
I'm playing air
guitar on FM
radio.

BIG BANG, SMALL BEACH

Given a universe emerging
from cold quiet, submerging
Into quiet cold,
it's easy to befriend
this sand,
embrace this heat
and dream the sounds
of sleep.

SKY SIGH

It's endemic to our species to gaze
at the night sky.
It began before the Stone Age
And will certainly continue.
We don't see the gods or our futures
above us.
We see a philosophy there, unarticulated
but nonetheless profound.
An expression of the value
of emptiness and an invitation
to be valuable with it.
Tonight, the pinnacle of evolution
turns the house lights off
on another day, goes outside
and accepts the invitation.
To everyone he's ever met,
he remains certainly, sacramentally
yours, if you can find him
in the dark.

PART TWO

AIRSCAPES

BIRTH DAZE

It happens every time they say
I have to make a wish: a drifting
darkness and recollection of Roman ruins.
After fifty, you can live inside your head,
envisioning the clearest night sky possible
on this planet, exploring the various meanings
of being completely cholesterol free.
The entire universe: a landscape much misprized
to which I frequently beg passage.
Angst: the conviction that this time
next year, I won't be in Tibet.

SATURDAY PSALTER

Old socialists sit Saturdays in Central Park,
wondering what happened to the revolution,
unable to believe Roosevelt was the closest
it came.
They tell each other, and the established banditry,
to remember Che's children will return.
A prophecy each week, again, fulfilled.

ST. TONY

Anthony beats the devil
at seminal devil games:
In a desert where tanks
would one day war,
he finds something
ineffable to love
the angel for.

RETIRED (ORLANDO)

Stalking peace by moon created
tidal pools, trying to recreate
the mystery of faith,
praying a liturgy of memories,
the celebrated psalms of age.

GOSPELS

Can wrens impart good news?
Can sparrows and starlings?
This frigid morning,
when they came for seed
I'd left them,
I grasped the exegetic beauty
of their faith:
the beneficence of finding food
in a safe place,
the chanted belief
that leaves and warmth
will return.

MISSED GIVINGS

The wind speaks to itself,
exulting in the company it keeps.
When I reach out, it vanishes.
How well we vanish, as if
vanishing were the reason
we appear.
The frontier was once everything
west of the Hudson.
Still, it seems the saddest
thing is lacking.

MOMENTARY PIECE

As a people, we have hardly excelled in the art of peace
but we believe we have.
It is a sublime illusion built on a sublime sublimation
of our history.
After all, we established and house the United Nations
and defeated the interpreters of Marx.
We created civil rights in the face of civil wrongs
and declared armed conflict on poverty.
We have done all we could to be fair.
We put the face of a Native American on a penny,
despite what he was thinking.
We expanded west until we reached the east
and realized we didn't belong there.
We lost a hot war, won a cold war and then tried our best
 to come home.
When I came home, I got profoundly lost
in the great state of Rhode Island.
I was praying my best to find Providence.

NEW MILLENNIUM BLUES

Done telling stories,
we suffer a moment
of truth:
Eye to eye,
life to life,
only calendars
and bartenders
change.

SOLOMON'S CITY

I went to Jerusalem without expectations
and came home hopes fulfilled.
Twenty centuries ago, this place
was in turmoil and remains so today.
What does this tell us about progress?
It says we progress while creating
and preserving ruins.
It says we have learned to live
with the disquieting lamentation
of widows.
It says the Temple will exist
as long as they continue to lament.

WOODSTOCK REVISITED

When the last of us die, the festival
will finally be over.
I'm being still but still passing by,
unable to enjoy the planetarium
at night.

STORMED

The river is swollen
with aspiration,
with deep tidal longings
and pelagic fantasies.
In its dreams it drowns
the stars.

UNSTRUNG

The sun rose early, light years
from Orion's belt.
My cat noticed it, then played
with string, his mind a universe
that sometimes includes me.

GAMBOLING

I don't believe in fate
but certainly there is chance,
so lets recuperate from being born,
lets stay alive, lets make it possible
to possibly be lucky,
for a while.

HIDDEN (OBVIOUSLY)

Stars, reaching out with the speed of light,
never know if anyone sees them.
The homeless, reaching out to anyone,
know they go unseen.
Tonight, I renew a vow to refuse to grasp
the meaning of success and revel in the joy
of having breathed a day invisibly away.

RETIRED

The temperature tonight is eleven degrees below freezing.
Here in upstate New York, the deer that survived
the hunting season are wondering why they bothered.
Some of the hunters are wondering why they're
still here too.
After Christmas, they live for next autumn's opening day.
In between, lots of talk about trophy bucks and the cost of
taxidermy.
I have trophies too. Laminated diplomas and certificates of
appreciation.
They attest to years of hunting before my license
expired and could never be renewed.
I'm left without work or vacations, guns or shells.
Just wall space and an abiding fear of taxidermists.

BEACHED

Out of work, love and touch.
Hermit monks and hermit crabs
dominate my dreams,
telling me it's almost pleasant
getting nowhere slow.
Awake, I must agree.

COLD WAR

Wake from a dream
in which promises
are broken:
black capped chickadees
in new night snow
by the shocked
and frozen
pond.

WINTERING

The frost and coming snow
will lock the earth.
Beside this hearthfire,
sea-pale visions, garnet
tales and plans.
The luxury of food.
The gem of warmth that generates
an unmolested sleep.

Find a drop of the ocean
in the drops of frozen,
falling rain.

Carry it safely home.

GROUND ZERO, ZERO GROUND

Another dangerous autumn has begun, the nurturer
of winter's dangerous coming.
Leaves will lose their mooring, summer's abundance of
anonynimity will end.
Incipient poets will declaim the beauty of incipient
change and of change itself while the planet
simply goes about its business.
Meanwhile, I have a checkbook to balance and a book
of prayers to pray and a great desire
to forget myself before putting both away.

PARSLEY, SAGE, ROSEMARY AND WINE

You burned every photo you had of us together
and every photo you could find of me alone.
I swear to you, truly, I'm easier than that
to forget.
Buddha directs us to empty ourselves
of who we think we are.
That's as simple as reliving four years
of college.
At sunrise, the Russians rushed westward
with open arms.
Nixon resigned this afternoon.
I'll be visiting Scarboro fair
to toast Mrs. Robinson and laminate
my diploma.

FRANCIS DREAMT

St. Francis of Assisi,
the Little Poor One,
heard a voice say
in his sleep,
"It takes surpassing grace
to laugh oneself to death."
Awake, he kissed the dawn,
caressed the day,
listened to the laughter
of creation.

ESPRESSO MOURNINGS

Angels have evaporated
and devils burnt
to ash.
I'm living to discover
when life becomes
a joke.

VALENTINE'S NIGHT

The distances between galaxies
and between each of us,
pronounced by being perceived.
Again, we realize lovers
are strangers too.
I retire to count the spare
change I've saved.

STELLAR RELATIONS

We send messages into space
to tell whoever my evolve
we are here, or once were,
then return to another day's
indifference, stoic as galactic
evolution and the distance
between stars.

THE PRICE OF EXPLORATION

They say it's cold from coast to coast
but colder in the heartland.
It's not the permanent permafrost
promised by nuclear winter,
but bitter enough to make
meditating memorable.
No great insights tonight, no satori
experiences, but a realization
of all I've lost and all
that's lost to me.
At dawn, I consider abiding mysteries:
arctic isolation and empathy
for the setting moon.
Perhaps things were better
before both of us were landed on.

THRICE REMOVED

There are people who find arctic isolation
in apartment buildings in the Bronx.
Others need the desert or high forest hiding.
All I need are the memories of what I've lost
and of all that's lost to me and the conviction
that this is the way it didn't have to be.

KEY WEST SATORI

As ocean and wave,
as desert and dune,
as God and the universe,
the universe and you:
not one but not two.

ANTIMATTERS

Before General Motors took over
the world,
there was air and oil.
Radioactivity made movie monsters
and everyone knew everything
about baseball.
Between commercials, the radio
proclaims the morning
too haiku.
I'm counseled to take tea
and see.
I'll see.

WINTER RETREAT

There's a chapel to meditate in
during the day
and Venus to watch the night
sky with
and time enough to understand
that these days peace
means piece.

ZEN FLYBY

Walking alone, autumn evenings, I'm tempted to
recall all that's lost to me.
A nighthawk strafes the footpath home,
uncaptured, purely mine.

PART THREE

GOOD DAZE, BAD DAYS

THIS MORNING

It's not that I didn't know all things must pass.
It's just that I've remembered I'm just passing.
This morning, I need a cup of black coffee
and no conversation to go with it.
A toast to old existentialists who took time
to take time seriously and consider
the mysteries that have befallen us.
A toast to anyone who wonders what's happened
to Bob Dylan?

BETTER GOOD FRIDAY

This deep Friday evening
my mind tries conceiving
the moment before
the Big Bang.
Vacuity birthing absence.
A no time of no thing
that had, from lack
of frustration, to dream
inevitable Christmas,
inevitable Easter,
inevitable silence
again.

GRACED

I have a friend who studies shadows.
Shadows, he believes, are epiphanies of Buddha.
They never grasp, they have no aspirations.
They simply are until they are gone.
Anarchical by nature, they die at sunset
in shadowy states of grace.

I know men, without homes, who sleep in their clothes.
They gather, at sunset, to chant sunset psalms,
to chant the songs and psalms of passing,
to honor holy transience and proclaim the mysteries
that have befallen them.
Thinner than light, they are the brothers of shadows.
Anarchical by nature, they have no need of grace.

My lover took months to die.
While waiting, she dreamt both sleeping and waking.
Anarchical by nature, she blessed the shadows
surrounding her,
gave thanks for the absence of a path to follow.
Passing gracefully, she bequeathed grace
and left me dreaming I could dream.

FM PRAYERS

The impoverished of spirit bless themselves
drinking morning coffee and dressing for the day.
In their hearts, they want to play where the deer and
antelope played and vanish where they vanished.
Until then, there's Woodstock rock on the radio
while inflation devalues the Beatitudes.

MEASURED MILES

A whitetail doe climbs the steps of my deck
to eat seeds put out for sparrows.
She has no idea of the history of loss
her species has endured.
There was a time when the frontier
began just across the Hudson.
Now I walk by that river,
in a country frontierless
from coast to coast.
At the end of my driveway,
I see Kerouac on the road.
He asks me if I can accept
the great embrace of highways?
He asks me if I know a way
he can avoid the tolls ?

LATE AUTUMN PASSING

Three does, followed by their buck,
search for food in the spent woods.
I'm motionless on Tarrytown Road,
having stopped my car, stopped thinking.
The deer move on, never noticing I noticed.

At home, a mandatory message in the mail;
best wishes from a woman I once loved.
It seems, somehow, we've been born again
as friends, caring for each other via notes
we sometimes send.

The sun withdraws, as planned.
Mourning doves chant mantras
with heroic nonchalance.
They love the way the world sounds.
They love the way the world is,
all evanescent as ever.

ONCE WISE

The pear tree in my garden
has never born fruit.
Like me, it must invent its purpose.
This spring, wed sparrows nested
on its strongest limb.
Is the tree fulfilled? A mystery,
seven times sealed.
This spring, I'm a person watching trees
and nesting sparrows.
Amazed that they cannot conceive
of any leafless time,
that they have faith in the abundance
of the season.
Amazed that once, when I was wise,
I thought there must be questions
to my answers.

(JELLY) ROLES

We must meet to mend our relationship.
We'll discuss current events, the fall
of Troy and life during the Dark Ages.
I'll pray an act of contrition, promising
to change my ways.
If you desert the Volunteers of America,
I'll never work on Maggie's farm again.
But I can still play Jefferson Airplane tapes
loud at night and on weekends
and you can still drink expresso
from a hot chocolate mug.
And we won't walk beaches at sunset
but will still hang out in SoHo.
And we'll both strike Valentine's Day
from our calendars and asterisk
the anniversary of the Russian Revolution.
And if we ever visit your mother together,
we'll be finally, forever in love.

APOCRYPHA

I was thinking apocalyptically,
when all four Beatles said they
wanted to hold my hand.
They told me to find
the bright side of things
and live like that side is real.
Otherwise, you end up
in a rented apartment on Patmos,
waiting with the Rolling Stones
for skies to open and days
to finally close.
St. John lived on Patmos.
He didn't sing or play guitar
but he rocked hard to the end.

KAMIKAZE

This December, I'll make a pilgrimage to Promenade Park
in Brooklyn.
From benches there, you can see across New York harbor
to all of the Manhattan skyline.
Years ago, when I worked in Brooklyn, I would walk
the park at lunch break.
I met one of the loves of my life there
and also one of my best friends.
Now I'll go to annihilate the differences
between my past and present.
I'll wear a cap backwards on my head
to show that I'm still cool.
I'll think about one way journeys people
who have had some success call bios.
I'll think about Christmas and about leaving
New York forever and about Navy pilots
who were airborne over the Pacific
when their carriers were sunk.
And I'll ask myself for the millionth time,
why I'm still looking into the illegible sky?

WARS END

A Vietnam vet and I were drinking off depressions
and reviewing reasons to be depressed.
In the heat of discussion and a Miami evening,
we realized a war isn't over until everyone
alive when it happened is dead.

SIXTIES SENSIBILITIES

Revolutionary reality has become evolutionary reality.
What our generation couldn't create,
future children will.
Meanwhile, we have gospel truth to profess:
Everything changes, over and again,
but someone, somewhere, signs you peace.

VIETNAM GENERATION BLUES

The mystery of the moon was solved
And hasn't been replaced.
King was killed, Kennedys were killed,
Merton was electrocuted turning on a fan.
Morrison had heart failure.
When the musics over, turn out
the lights,
and when the war is over,
forget about it.
There comes a time, beautiful friend,
when you know too much of knowing;
when you fish the Sea of Galilee
and throw back everything you catch.

RED BURIAL BLUES

A grave message
From a grave place:
Wasted does as wasted is.
And I ask myself,
What happened in Bolivia?
Where is Che?

GOOD NIGHT WEATHER

No one reads or hears about Laotians anymore
or about the proximity of Havana to Miami.
There haven't been any new lysergic acid
studies and none of my friends wrote novels.
So, before retiring, I insist on seeing
the night's moonlit snow.
It's almost a whiter shade of pale
and always cooler than really cool.

HOLOCAUST

I was talking angrily, spent and dismayed, to God
about the Holocaust.
He said He had nothing to do with it
and silently left the room.
Later, He returned six million times,
ashen, gasping for air.

PEACE OUT

Auschwitz, Bataan, My Lai,
expressions of a statement
primates evolved to make:
"We were here, look what we
were able to do."

THE ELECT

I wonder what Nixon thinks about, quiet and alone?
Does he fantasize about honor and finally being
understood?
Does he open the door to China over and over again?
Does he think he's a dream that's become
a documentary?
Is he willing to testify that anyone real
has ever really been elected?

NIXON GIRLS

Those sullen, moon clad women
I was fond of asked for nothing
but my life and more Saigons
to save.
They passed into history
nurturing families and plans
to assassinate Fidel,
still wondering, over cake
and beer, why Watergate
was wrong?

GENETIC DRIFT

Eggs are hatching on the Croton River
into water and wind.
Friends and I observe new life
join the daily fire:
unremitting readiness
uselessly united,
ultimately nothing
we've heard a rumor of.

VIGIL, NEVADA TEST SITE

We gather to honor blessed evanescense,
to chant the songs and psalms of passing,
to celebrate the wisdom of cold stone
and the sagacity of high desert.
We meet to remember that the lives
of monks and poets are important
because they are purposely irrelevant
and to mark the value of our lack
of stocks and bonds.
We come here to wonder why people believed
they must be able to destroy all of creation
in order to save the world?
We come here to wonder why would
have done it?

EASTER MORNING PSALM

This daybreak is a promise kept,
a chanted promise, rising.
Each mote of dust shall rise, is rising,
all fear, all doubt, all sorrow, rising.
We will remember, God will remember,
to sanctify spent tears.
Then God will weep no more,
for we shall have stopped weeping.

ABOUT THE AUTHOR

Michael Maiello, a native New Yorker, is a graduate of St. John's University, City University of New York and St. John's University School of Law.

He has served as an administrator at Catholic Charities, Diocese of Brooklyn and as executive director of Catholic Family and Community Services, Diocese of Paterson, N.J. He has also served as director of social services, Diocese of Paterson. He has written several essays and articles as well as the book *Sacred Moments, Holy Days*.